Some Folks Like Cats

Some Folks Like Cats

and Other Poems

by Ivy O. Eastwick

Compiled by Walter B. Barbe, Ph.D.
Illustrations by Mary Kurnick Maass

Wordsong · Boyds Mills Press

For Marilyn

— W. B. B.

For Les

— M. K. M.

Text copyright © 2002 by Highlights for Children, Inc.
Illustrations copyright © 2002 by Mary Kurnick Maass

Published by Wordsong
Boyds Mills Press, Inc.
A Highlights Company
815 Church Street
Honesdale, Pennsylvania 18431
Printed in China

U.S. Cataloging-in-Publication Data
(Library of Congress Standards)

Eastwick, Ivy O.
Some folks like cats : and other poems / by Ivy O. Eastwick ;
compiled by Walter B. Barbe ; illustrations by Mary Kurnick Maass.— 1st ed.
[32] p. : col. ill. ; cm.
Summary: Lighthearted and humorous poetry
about things real and imagined.
ISBN: 1-56397-450-9
1. Humorous poetry, American — Juvenile literature. 2. Children's
poetry, American. [1. Humorous poetry. 2. American poetry.]
I. Barbe, Walter B.   II. Maass, Mary Kurnick.   III. Title.
811.54 21 2002   CIP
2001088728

First edition, 2002
Book designed by Jason Thorne and Mary Kurnick Maass
The text of this book is set in 16-point Cochin.

Visit our Web site at www.boydsmillspress.com

10 9 8 7 6 5 4 3 2 1

Contents

Introduction

Ivy Eastwick was my friend. Over the years, we exchanged many letters. I enjoyed receiving hers for two reasons. First, I never knew what country her letters would come from, for she lived all over the world. And second, in every letter she enclosed several of her poems. I believe I knew her well. By reading these poems, I hope you will get to know her and that she will be one of your friends, too.

WALTER B. BARBE

Nonsense and Humor

Mice's Song

Cheese on toast
  delights us most.
Please leave a little
  beneath the table.
Crackers and cheese
  are sure to please,
And we shall eat
  as much as we're able.
Cheeseless food
  is not so good,
But if we're hungry
  we wouldn't mind it.
Whatever's to spare
  please leave it where
It's easiest for
  us mice to find it.

Some Folks Like Cats

Some folks like cats.
Some folks don't.
Some folks will talk to cats.
Some folks won't.
Some folks admire cats and love
their purrrrrrrrrrrrrrrrrrrrrrrr,
while some folks shudder at the
touch of their furrrrrrrrrrrrrr.
Oh, my aunt Maria shrieks higher
and higher when my cat, Jeremiah,
rubs up against herrrrrrrrrrrrrrrrrr.

Old Mr. Medlicott

A funnier sight
I never did see
than old Mr. Medlicott
chasing a bee.

The funniest sight
I ever did see
was old Mr. Medlicott
chased by a bee.

Fun

A moving staircase
is truly fun,
you need not walk,
you need not run,
you just stand still —
it's like a game —
and you get to the top floor
just the same.

House for Rent

House for rent.
Greenacre Wood.
Lovely views.
Location good.
Tiny bedroom.
Teeny hall.
Kitchen with oven,
pots, pans, and all.
Well-stocked larder
with things for cooking.
Parlor window
that's overlooking
a gurgling brook
and mossy pillows,
and woodpeckers pecking
in pussy willows.

House for rent
to a good little gnome
who needs a place
to call his home.

Nature's World

Jane and the Birds

Jane
loves the owl call,
Jane
loves the lark,
Jane
loves all birds from
the morning till dark.
Jane
loves to watch them
in flight from the lawn —
the owl in the evening,
the skylark at dawn.
Jane
wakes so early,
the moment it's light,
and won't go to sleep till
the owl calls

"GOOD NIGHT."

The Friendly Robin

The friendly robin
from his tree
comes flying, flying
down to me,
and when I give him
crumbs to eat,
rewards me with
a song most sweet.

Me and the Sunflowers

Oh, Sunflowers,
you are twelve feet high
and very, very tall,
while I am only
six years old
and really rather small.
But see the sun
which beams down
through the skies
all bright and blue—
oh, YOU must seem
as small to him
as I seem small
to YOU.

Very Tall!

The Violet
is one inch tall,
the Cowslip
measures two,
the Bluebell
is three inches
(its top inch is
deepest blue),
the Hollyhock
in pink silk frock
is taller
than them all—
it grows
  and grows
    and grows
      and GROWS
until it's
      SIX
        FEET
          TALL!

Rabbit

It's a habit
of Rabbit
to leap in the sun,
to dance in
deep clover,
to jump and have fun
over hillock
and tussock
and thornbush and bramble—
for a rabbit
will leap
where a tortoise will amble.

Seasons and Weather

Hello, April

"Hello, April,
good-bye, March,"
sing the maple,
birch, and larch.

"Hello, Rainbow,
hello, Spring,
hello, Blackbird,
caroling.

"April's coming.
April's here,
April, loveliest
of the year."

Wind

Nobody knows
where the Wind goes —
it comes with a flutter
it goes with a gust,
it comes when it will
and it goes where it must
but —
where it goes,
nobody knows.

Seven Raindrops

I counted seven drops of rain—
they spattered on my windowpane,
then lay like diamonds on the sill
and stayed there, bright and shining,
                                    till
the sun came up above the hill.

I watched it rise—it was so bright
it touched the treetops all with light,
and when I looked down once again,
gone were my seven drops of rain.

The Autumn Leaves

Green and yellow,
Gold and brown,
The autumn leaves
Come dancing down,
Blown from their swaying,
Laughing trees
By a dancing, prancing,
Merry young breeze.
Here they come
Down the village street,
Past the children's
Running feet.
Here, by the streamlet!
There, by the hill!
The autumn leaves
Will never stand still.

One Thing I Know

Snow's cold.
Snow's white.
Snow's soft.
Snow's bright.
One thing
I know—
I   DO
LIKE   SNOW.

Wishes, Dreams, and Fancy

A Sound and Touch of Nothing

Softer than a moth's wing,
lighter than a sigh,
who was it
and
what was it
that just went by?

Enough to Eat

My second cousin Marguerite
can never get enough to eat.
Pies and patties, jelly, jam,
chicken roast or honey ham,
pastry—flaky, short, or puff—
she simply cannot get enough
and says that candies, chocolate creams,
cakes, and biscuits fill her dreams.

My Valentine Gift

My own true love,
my valentine,
accept this little
gift of mine.
It's tied with ribbon,
not with string,
it is a very
precious thing—
it is a song
for you to sing.

My Cousin and I

"To whom are you waving?"
My cousin said to me.

"I'm waving to a mermaid
Who's swimming in the sea."

"To whom are you talking?"
My cousin said to me.

"I'm talking to the white horse
Which gallops on the sea."

She did not see the mermaid;
She did not see the horse.

And all because she did not
Believe in them, of course.

Polly Peppercorn

Young Polly Peppercorn
Sat in the rain
Waiting for sunshine
To come round again.
Cloud upon cloud
Upon cloud floated by—
Young Polly Peppercorn
Sighed a huge sigh.

Drip! drip! drip! it fell,
Drop after drop,
Just as though
It never would stop.
It soaked Polly's stockings
Right down to her toes,
It trick-trickled down
Her little snub nose.

Drenched and dripping,
Poor Polly sat
While the rain came down
With a *pitter-pit-pat*
Like the feet of mice
On the floor at night.
And there wasn't a single
Glimmer of light.

Never mind, Polly.
Now, never mind, dear!
Tomorrow's another day—
'Twill soon be here.
Tomorrow's a sunny day—
Bright as can be—
It's just round the corner,
So wait here with me.